To Anne

Raymond

SCENES FROM SEASONS

But Not That Sort of Season

Tom East

Tom East

Benybont Books

https://www.benybont.org/
First published 2019
Copyright © Tom East, 2019

ISBN 978-1-9164942-8-2

To Suki, Joseph, Edmund, Ping and Annabella

ACKNOWLEDGEMENTS
Most of these poems have been previously published in magazines like *CAMBRIA*, *ORBIS*, *OTHER POETRY*, *OUPOSTS*, *ROUNDYHOUSE* and *STAPLE*. A few appeared in an earlier collection, now out-of-print, *NIETZSCHE'S CHILDREN*.

Tom East

CONTENTS

A Prayer

O Lord of Our Days,
save us from the standard-setters;
the hush-voiced counsellors;
the inspectors; the auditors;
the therapists and the charterers;
the petition-makers;
the ethical advisers.

Please keep us from the clutches
of all doctors, lawyers and accountants.
Spare us the priests and law-makers:
(anyone in a long black gown).
Close our ears to the lying politicians.

Let us creep softly into fat-arsed middle age
without the child within withering away.
And when our minds become fuddled with years,
or drink, or straitened thoughts,
keep a few crystals of truth
alive in some bright corner.
Let not madness, nor yet cold sanity
overtake us.

And when the time comes
to switch off the light,
Do it quickly.

But not just yet.

The Father of my Uncle

Yes, I recall my uncle's father, the old man in the chair.
He had white dusty hair
and died when I was three,
as if he'd never been there.

He'd sit all day in the dark parlour
regarding the world with disfavour
and not a single trace of humour.

He wore a brown tobacco-smelling suit,
though I never saw him with a light
and I never saw him smoke.
He never shared a joke;
I never heard him speak.
Could be he'd lost the touch;
perhaps in all those years he'd seen too much.

We had no ties of blood:
his grandsire had crossed the sea from far Tralee,
a place where no roses grow;
and where even the life-giving potato
had rotted in the mud.

The old man had left a London slum
for the Rhondda, with his gin-soaked wife
and my uncle, in those days his toddler son,
because he'd heard the streets were paved with coal
but all he'd found was grief and strife
and there he grew old.

One day, he rose from his seat near the mantel
to stumble down the passageway.
Amazed to find he could move at all,
I followed him, until he fell back upon me.

My mother screamed: 'He's killed him!'
I thought: 'I've killed him.'
But my mother was thinking of me;
she thought the old man had put out my light.

But maybe I was right:
the father of my uncle died when I was three.

Poem to Spring

Spring:

>   when the Lion roars among the stars;
>   when a quickness moves across the fields;
>   when days themselves give more to us.

How do I know these things?

>   Not from the dust of books;
>   nor from the hard school bench;
>   still less because the preacher tells me so.

No, I know because I know.

>   Because my eyes see the Lion;
>   because I walk across those fields;
>   because I have time for these things.

But:

>   when my eyes see just a line of stars;
>   when only title deeds grow in the fields;
>   when there is time just to walk the straight line:

then winter comes.

Scenes from a Season of Pop Festivals

[I] Isle of Wight Pop Festival, 2015

On the Monday morning after,
they trooped through Portsmouth Harbour Station.
Anoraks, tents, guitars, babies
borne by backpacking weekenders.

Flush-faced females;
fiercer males with bristles or beards;
those in middle-years,
reliving forty-five year old purple haze.

Some wore sandals, some careful casuals;
a few bare feet padded the platform;
one young man brazened a Glastonbury mud-film on his boots;
a badge of honour, though the weather had been fine.

These were moments to lift an aging heart
on a warm summer's day.
When simple sights like these
leave it cold and lying,
then the chill mists of winter cling.

[II] Blondie at Glastonbury

You've still got it, Debbie Harry.

Some loss of grace about the waist,
those baby-reins, white on black trouser suit,
the stillness of your standing.
They don't tell the truth.

You've still got it, Debbie.

Lively ladies with long memories relive nineteen-eighty
on the shoulders of young men,
living for the moment.

And what is it you've got?
Eyelids smouldering with pearl?
Silver vowels to lighten the night?
Timing and rhythm, stylish precision?

But, as you step back on the stage,
to let the drummer drum his mood,
I see you don't know, either
and neither should you care.

Girl on a Train

She shouldn't have looked at me in that way.
      Not with my wife sitting there.
Flashing her smile, flickering eyes of grey
      and tossing her long, blonde hair.

It'd been a long time since a girl of her age
      looked at me quite so boldly,
with a promise to set my blood in a rage,
      so I smiled back, warmly, not coldly.

And when my wife left for the buffet,
      then she spoke, sweet and low.
She told me she was born at Christmas, so 'Holly'.
      She told me she had a sister called 'Jo'.

She told me she'd been twenty-three years on this Earth;
      she told me of all the places she'd seen;
she told me her mother had a difficult birth,
      and she'd been sent to a special school in East Dean.

And when my wife returned still she spoke, and kept talking
      as the train rumbled on from Romsey to Bath.
It was of her life she was speaking:
      we numbered her cousins, uncles and aunts.

We learned of her kin, her pets and her boyfriend,
      whose picture she held in her trembling hand.
We learned of her hopes and her dream to extend
      a life to us strange, remote and so bland.

And at Bath we had to remind this lost child,
      to rejoin quiet life with her mother at home.
'It's nice to meet new people,' she said,
      smiling sadly, as she turned to go.

The Perseids at 3am

Night fishing; bright meteors.
Star-trails streak black sky:
one, two, three, four and more.

Companions drowse, while I lie alone:
just me, the dark dome in its dream
and timeless space spinning slowly.

An owl hoots its feathered fear,
saying she alone is lady of this lake;
I lie the interloper here.
Yet the stars above are all I seek.

Y Perseids am Dri o'r Gloch y Bore

Pysgota'r nos; ser wîb disglair.
Llusgo ser yn rhesu'r awyr du:
un, dau, tri, pedwar a mwy.

Cyfeillion sy'n cysgu, tra bo fi'n gorwedd ar fy mhen fy hun:
dim ond fi, y gromen dywyll yn ei breuddwyd
a gofod heb amser yn troi'n araf.

Mae tylluan yn hwtio ei hofn pluog,
yn dweud taw hithau yn unig yw merch y llyn hwn;
a bo fi'n gorwedd, yr ymwthiwr yma.
Ond y ser uwchben yw pobeth dw i'n dymuno.

Cyfiethiad Joyce James

In the National Gallery

In a sombre room,
marked by umbers and ochres,
Doubting Thomas thrust a hand
into his Leader's side.

I thought: 'I don't believe that'.

In the Impressionists' Hall
marked by lyrics of light,
Lake Keitele's mirrored surface
drew us in.

I thought: 'I believe this.'

Seventeen and Twenty-one

She a woman, twenty-one;
I a callow seventeen.
From lips warm as summer wine,
I took just youth's illusion.

Somewhere Near Merthyr

'Come to my bridal party;
Both of you come. It's not too far.
You won't be sorry;
others you know will be there.

We're just a few miles from Merthyr.
I'll draw you a plan.'
So, on the date we travelled together,
aided by lines on her map.

We drove up the A470;
past Quaker's Yard and
mining's other legacy,
through the rain and the wind.

The sketch was poor;
the streets all looked the same
but at last we found the Memorial Hall
in the midst of the fog and the haze.

Inside, she still wore her white;
standing by a plaque that numbered the dead;
her bright smile at odds with the dark night.
'But this is –' 'Yes,' she said.

'That was then. This is my wedding day.'
Sixteen years before, she'd lost five friends and a father
as Pantglas School was swept away,
though not her life, nor that of her brother.

So, we danced the night away
with our second son, to be born the next year
in a warmer, safer place
and allowed purer air.

To me, Aberfan is a black-and-white story;
black because of young lives
lost in a sweep of shameful slurry;
white because of a bright smile lighting a dark night.

Which do I remember best,
after all these years?
The history or a wedding dress?
It is not for me to say; that right is theirs.

Yet I can picture a beguiling smile
on the night she put away her childhood hell
and, through life's darkest veil,
I hope she's smiling still.

Scenes from Fishing Seasons

[I] January Pike

The leafless trees shriek
in answer to the wrecking wind.

Nothing else bites in the frost-bitten morning;
nothing else moves in the pre-dawn air; the ice-bound water
only me and my grinning quarry;
the knifing pike with his wolfish jaws.

Needle teeth torment tiddlers:
this shark of the lake makes his mark around the bay;
a flash and a slash and flesh flakes away.

A silver spinner shams a sick fish;
a heavy heave and the pike learns the hook.
There is tightened line, heightened life
as the killer is bound for bank.

It's only then I learn
that a fish out of water
is no demon from some deep reign.
It's a waterless creature.

[II] Early Morning Fishing

We take the train to Maidenhead
to get us to the Thames at setting sun.
A couple of casts to careless chub
then it's time to wrap in newsprint,
to store some shreds of summer heat
against the biting night.

There's a darkness you can touch;
a stillness you can't judge.
Water-voles shrill around you,
shrieking to their mates, while speaking to your soul.

Then, before dawn comes,
the mist creeps from the river and seeps into your bones,
no need here of alarms.
                    And so the day begins.

In the Particular Circumstances

I saw them on the morning train,
  judging them to be two bankers,
  or perhaps a pair of corporate accountants,
  each out to impress the other.

  Snatches of their conversation
  intrude upon my bleared senses:
  'in the particular circumstances
  of which you speak, and
  having regard to the environmental influences...'

                    Can people really talk like that?

I saw them on the evening train,
  two suits full of tiredness;
  their day's work done;
  a few creases in their carefully presented images.

  No strident conversation now
  to disturb my evening peace.
  Their murmuring voices only
  tell wearily of some mundane defeat.

                    Can people really live like that?

  Well, in the particular circumstances, and
  having regard to the environmental influences,
                    it seems that they can.

Stones

Wandsworth. Scenes from my youth.
You'd have to say it's better.
The old house, with its cracked bath,
has a new, expensive one poured in as a neighbour.
(London property prices and rents.)

'The Mascot', once the home of sticky sweets,
now stocks fine art prints.
The launderette today sells smart antiques.

But here's one thing that looks as staunch:
the old Huguenot burial ground,
so oddly sited next to the Catholic church
of St Mary Magdalene the Beloved.

To walk the crooked footpath between the two
gave me shivers sixty years ago.
As if human remains, in defiance of nature's law,
could rise up and shift the heavy stones.

Where are Jacques Monibot, Georges Issy and Henri Tissard?
Their very names, etched proudly for three centuries of hope,
have been worn away by half a century of modern times.
The acid rain has stronger magic than the stones.

Body Language

They sat three seats ahead.
 He with shaven scalp and a profile aching with aggression;
 she with averted gaze and more modest bearing.

I couldn't hear his hectoring tones,
 though saw his lips moving with animation,
 and imagined the spleen in his words.
She nodded vigorously to keep the peace,
 looking fixedly out of the bus window.

I invented whole biographies for them.
 He some latter-day Punch, his slapstick at home;
 she a modern Judy, meekly accepting all he cared to throw;
 in the house a Baby Punchinello, to be tossed around.

We hurried on for half-a-mile, then
 his lips twitched
 and drew back in a smile.
 Her shoulders shook with laughter.
 She turned to him and smiled.
I'd got it all so wrong.

Echoes through Milk Wood

How can one man's words enter the soul of another?
If that man were a magician with pencil and wash
would he make an album of Organ Morgan and Polly Garter?
>   He would through Dylan's art.
>   Ask Peter Blake.

Can a poem flow through blue notes on a saxophone
in some starless and a Bible-black night of the mind?
>   It can with Dylan's art.
>   Ask Stan Tracey.

Why don't we all strive to imitate
the cadences, the images, the resonances
of this man from the ugly, lovely town?
>   It wouldn't be Dylan's art.
>   Ask who you like.

Heritage Park

'Never thought I'd be a tourist guide,' he said,
'but at least my fingernails stay clean
　　　showing folk around the old pit-head.
　　　It's good to have a job at all, the Missus said.

This is where my father would have been
　　　at just this time of day, or near enough.
He was foreman of the winding-room. And Duw, he was mean.
Electric drives this now, for you. Then, it was steam.

　　　As a way to earn a crust, I tell you it was tough:
I could give you scores of names of them that died
　　　of dust. Aye, a lot of that, and it was rough:
　　　filthy, choking, nasty stuff.

Yes, there were some things I never could abide,
　　　and it's true what the Missus said:
I've got a job; I've got some pride.
But I never thought I'd be a tourist guide.'

Life on Lock's Common

Hot sun rolling streams of sweat
    down my brow to my cheek,
I stopped for a moment,
    feeling superior to lazier brethren at my feet.

I'd stretched my limbs on a coastal walk;
    they'd only stretched theirs in the sun.
My salt was gained on a healthy task;
    theirs only because the sun shone.

Then I looked down at a silver path:
    a slug, struggling through the heat of the afternoon,
trailing his life and his death
    in a sheen of drying slime.

Soon to be no more than a husk for hungry birds,
    or a scrap to be swept away by the evening wind,
still he maintained his stubborn slide towards
    nothing but a mucoid madness end.

I wiped the sweat from my brow,
    poured water freely down my throat
and, feeling superior no more,
      soldiered on through the heat.

The Seven Lies of Man

(No woman would behave in this way)

One

Pink, chubby, much-loved infant,
you lie there, mewling and puking.
Still, it won't be long now before:

Two

The best schoolboy days
are when you lie there in the heather,
dreaming dreams of the days to come.
And, after this, the best days
are when you dream of the days that have been.

Three

Oh, to lie there in her arms;
to feel her soft, warm breasts
easing into your anger.
As a lover you'll do anything for this.

Four

Now you've got the lie of the land,
you've got it made.
Just wait, soldier.
You'll conquer all;
you'll show them.

Five

In the search for truth
you sometimes have to tell a lie.
So, the more lies you tell,
the more you should be admired.
Justice should be done.

Six

I cannot tell a lie, Pantaloon.
Nobody is charmed by your hairy ears,
your public farts, or your picking of nose at table.
As you like it it may be,
but no one else does.

Seven

And now you're in the last days of your second childhood.
You lie there, mewling and puking.
Still, it won't be long now before –

[Jacques, in **As You Like It***, II vii, said that the Seven Ages of Man were: (1) Infant; (2) Schoolboy; (3) Lover; (4) Soldier; (5) Justice; (6) Pantaloon; (7) Second Childhood.]*

London Welsh

1: London

'Caewch y drws!'
'Mae hi'n bwrw glaw.'
'Bara chaws a chwrw.'
I thought these were things English people said;
didn't understand why they laughed in school,
nor when I said 'thruppence'.

The place that my mother called 'down home'
only awoke paint-box images
of steep streets and hills at the end of a cloud:
slate-grey, misty green, and always wet.

Where did my father learn this foreign speech
that he sometimes spoke swiftly with his brothers?
Not often: even the dog tipped its head
when he slipped his tongue so easily
around the strange consonants.

Later, I didn't mind.
I was different, I was Welsh.

2: Wales

And now I live in Wales.
I've been here for forty years.

I've visited the bleak uplands
where my people scratched their living.
I've seen worn headstones:
'Ffarwel blant a ffarwel briod,
Ffarwel bopeth yn y byd.'
I know the names of Llywelyn,
Glyndŵr, and even Mari Jones.

'Ah, but you're not really Welsh, are you?'
says some Smith or Brown from Treorchy,
whose grandfather followed the coal in nineteen-ten.

But I don't really mind.
I'm different: I'm a Cockney.

Scenes from a Season of War Graves

[I] My Uncle Charles, 1894-1915

Chocques: the Graveyard
For thirty years I'd wanted to be here.
You'd think I'd have felt more:
at least a lump in the throat to go
to this place where the brother my father never knew
had left his lonely shadow.

But no; my uncle's was just one in neat rows
of well-tended white stones.
One was to mark the short life of a boy
who'd left his family, lying about his seasons;
another was for an elder sergeant who'd left a widow
by seeing his duty in simple visions.

There were Indians and Chinese who'd toiled,
with a shovel instead of a Lee-Enfield.
They probably didn't know why they were there;
if they even knew where they were.
There were soldiers from England, Scotland, and Ireland.
Even a stray German lay there as a friend.

Only the family name
gave my uncle's grave a different form.

Festubert: the Battlefield
A potted plant duly placed,
we went to see the green field
where one day in a summerless May
he was one of seven hundred who'd heard the whistle's sound
and left their lives in the mud.

It wasn't so green in the pre-dawn blackness when
machine-gun bullets and shells
whipped the ground and ripped through flesh
for the prize of another hundred mired yards to be held.

Béthune: the City
The city is a reclaimed ghost;
it looks rooted in centuries past.
You wouldn't know the church where I lit the candle
was once no more than a heap of rubble.

It was there I asked 'why did he die?'
For the King's Shilling? For ideas?
For the Army tot of rum? *Pro patria mori*?
For the crest of the Royal Welch Fusiliers? For his butties?

No, it wasn't really for any of these
that his was one of a million murders.
He died because
he was following the orders

of someone who knew better,
who was following the orders,
of someone who knew better,
and knew he was God's defender.

[II] Rifleman 47041

Over the bridge from Glanrhyd Hospital
there is a long-grassed field.
Officially, it's 'Bridgend Mental Hospital Cemetery',
though there's only one stone to be seen:
that of a shell-shocked soldier of the Great War.

Approaching the marker of Rifleman 47041,
CW Murphy of the Monmouthshire Regiment,
(no name, just initials),
you all at once realise that you're walking upon the bones of
others,
not important enough to have their passing signed,
even in wood, by someone doing a job.

A shiver runs through you at this sudden knowledge;
and another when you stand before the last resting place of
Rifleman 47041,
looking at the mass-produced crosses and paper flowers,
just wondering why.

Is it better to lie in a well-tended war grave,
or in an anonymous, unmarked grassed plot
in a mental hospital?
Not much of a choice, is it?
Especially when you have to go through hell
to get there.

[III] Edmund Baton, 1931-1945

It's pleasant here at Huisnes-sur-Mer,
a green mound of flower and shrub,
until you reach the ring of stone,
the concrete mausoleum.

Born in the wrong year;
living in the wrong place;
dying among the wrong people;
lying now among the soldiers;
this son of the vanquished victors.

Denied his youth;
denied the life-giving crust;
denied any requiem but the whistling wind;
denied even a few feet of French soil.

Young bones locked in a block of concrete
can give no laughing warning
of those sombre, war-clad years
to his children, or to theirs.

But then it was his side
that marched the streets of France.
His fathers were the ones who took their women.
This was the child raised to the sound of war parades.

An eye for an eye;
a tooth for a tooth;
a life for a life;
a child for a child;
a hate for a hate.

That's why twelve thousand lie here,
entombed, not to touch the ground,
shouldering the burden of a nation's shame.
And he shall bear his child's share.

Mr Jaksó, Instant Brit

Of course I said, 'yes, you can sit there'.
It was only the canteen, not worth a fuss.
And he said he wanted to talk, to hear from another.
'Of course,' I said. 'Yes.'

He asked if I'd heard of Russian tanks in Budapest;
he told me how he'd fled from his city in fear,
but now wanted to be just like us.

Though he was called 'Mr Jaksó,' wouldn't that matter?
Would 'Jackson' sound more like a British success?
And, to a shame that still burns across all these years
of course I said, 'Yes'.

Digging for Peace

They were digging for peace
as ten years before they'd dug for victory.
    We watched them,
    neither understanding nor caring,
    more interested in the small explosions
    from our cap guns.

Slowly, patiently, they dug
    tilling the earth, rebuilding the world.
    A pile of sticks was added to daily;
    a symbol of the returning order.

Suddenly, from a blue suburban sky,
    came a brief whirlwind.
    It tossed the sticks thirty feet in the air.
    They made a loud report, like a pistol shot.
    The men ran for cover
    as they'd done in the war.

We laughed.

Letter from Chile

So, Gloria Casanueva Coke,
Five years since from across the seas you wrote
    With news that bridged the generations.
    Your letter was heavy with emotion,
In learning that we had some common blood
From old great-grandfather, errant and proud,
    Casting his seed across two continents
    With not a thought or care for consequence.

Please write back soon, you said; of course I did
With a letter bright, a letter candid.

And two more into silence followed on:
Chilean embassy said no such person.

Carta de Chile

Entonces, Gloria Casanueva Coke,
Cinco años desde que escribiste a través de los mares
Con noticias que tendieron un puente a generaciones.
Tu carta estaba cargada de emoción,
Al saber que teniamos alguna sangre común
Del viejo bisabuelo, errante y orgulloso,
Arrojando sus semillas a lo largo de dos continentes
Sin consideración ni cuidado por la consecuencia.

Por favor escribe pronto, dijeste; por supuesto que lo hice
Con una carta viva, una carta sincera.

Y dos mas siguieron en silencio:
Embajada chilena dijo no hay tal persona.

(En español para Matías Serra Bradford)

The Shadow in the Corner

At the age of four or five
I used to watch spiders disappearing into
the shadows in the corner.
I thought that they were hurrying home
to their monster mother:
a venom-dripping creature from that otherworld.

I was afraid to go to sleep,
thinking this hag from the gloom,
would emerge from her witching lair,
entwine me in her hairy legs,
and feast upon my flesh.
But she never did.

Growing up, though still a child,
I was blessed or cursed
with a high and hot imagination.
Skulls would scream at me
from the walls of my night.

The tilt of a tombstone;
dark dreams of death;
the shadows in the corner;
all told their own tales.
But they never came true.

Later, pretending to be a man,
I learned to put away childish fears
along with childish things.
But still there lingered
some shameful secret:
fears of a shadow shaping itself in the corner,
taking on solid essence, stepping out,
and claiming me for its own.
But it never did.

Tom East

Now those days are gone.
I swing spiders from their spindly legs;
I scoff at stories of screaming skulls;
I smile at secret fears of shades.
And the only dark place I fear
is the shadow in the corner
of my mind.

Herman Melville

I

So, Herman, what demons swim through your mind
that you make a monster of a harmless mammal,
singing to its fellows in the depths of the sea?

Why did you people your *Pequod* with
scarred sailors and scared savages;
why did you press your pages with
twisted scriptures and sea spirits,
making us call *you* Ishmael?

II

Or is it we who are denied
dreams born of dwelling by the deep ;
of truths torn from
seasons on the restless strand between sea and shore?

Not knowing Nantucket,
do we not know our natures?
What it must be to pit puny men
against the wrath of the waves.

A hand-held harpoon
or an enfolding cocoon?

Poem for the Cider-Bench

On my cider-bench
    I can taste *The Golden Apples of the Sun*;
    watch butterflies lilting by on woven wings;
    see spiders spinning their silken spells.

On my cider-bench
    I can see *A Fair Field Full of Folk*,
    waving and smiling as they go about their business,
    each willing to help the other.

On my cider-bench
    I will be joined by Irving and the two Williams.
    We shall toast the power of the pen:
    mightier than the sword and the neutron-bomb.

And where is my cider-bench?
    Locked away in the vaults of Queen Camilla
    at the bottom of my garden,
    where it's a summer-long *White Christmas*
    and the fairies play all day.

Notes

[1] William Langland, W(illiam) B(utler) Yeats and Irving Berlin are the writers of *The Song of Wandering Aengus*, *The Vision Concerning Piers Plowman* and *White Christmas*, from which works the quotations are taken.
[2] We are assured there'll never be a Queen Camilla.

Scenes from a Season of Artwork

[1] The Worth of a Lowry

'It's like selling the family silver,'
says the outraged Leader of the Tories.
'Our heritage should be preserved.
We owe it to the Citizens of Bury.'

The cost of that heritage
is a score or more of home-helps;
a dozen teachers;
maybe half a new road;
or a pound on the rents.

Lawrence Stephen Lowry
would have liked that half-million.
His family would not then have needed
to move from respectable Victoria Park
to the grimy industry of Pendlebury.

He might then have been able to paint
still-lives and flowers.
No need for the thud of steam-hammers;
the *clackety-clack* of the shuttle on loom;
the clump of a thousand hob-nail boots
as they marched to the mill in the morning.

'It's because of the budget deficit,'
says the Labour Leader.
'But the eight million pounds worth
of Victorian Art are safe with us.
We'll never touch them.'

[In February, 2006 Bury Council announced that it was to sell a Lowry painting
valued at half-a-million pounds to help meet a budget deficit].

[II] John Drewe and the Meaning of Art

John Myatt is a Master
somewhat in the cast of the Old Ones
(or at least he copied their work
with KY Jelly and carpet-sweepings).
Now he's hanging in The Tate.

The experts and auctioneers are Money-men
rather in the style of so many others
who trade in stocks and shares.
(It's just that their holdings are nicer to see).
They've really been hung out to dry.

John Drewe is a True Artist,
a Phineas T. Barnum kind of guy,
forging evidence with a fibre-tip pen;
forging trust with a few free lunches.
And they'd hang him if only they could.

John Drewe was gaoled for six years in February, 1999, convicted of fraud and
other charges. He sold copies of 'Old Masters' created by John Myatt (gaoled for
a year). Drewe gained the confidence of the arts establishment with a few simple
courtesies and by giving the appearance of being 'one of their own kind'.

[iii] The Garden of Hieronymous Bosch

Won't you come inside my Garden of Earthly Delights?
        See my mind release its burden;
see Heaven to left and Hell to right.
        Won't you come inside my garden?

        See the ghouls swarm in their legion;
see goblin's claw and impish bite;
        see virgin mate with cacodaemon;

see the foul fiend in delight;
        see and share my starless vision;
see brightest day as darkest night.
        Won't you come inside my garden?

Sugarcandy Mountain

My introduction to Romania
was a stone-faced customs official,
searching through my luggage
for non-existent Bibles.

He needn't have bothered;
Moses the Raven had landed centuries before
to tell his tales
of Sugarcandy Mountain.

A few days later
in Minastaria Snagov
I had a halting conversation
with a priest of the Orthodox Church.

From his lips fell words of Romanian, German and English;
in his eyes was a dream of faraway Sugarcandy Mountain;
in his hands he held a cup of cool well water;
that might have come from Sugarcandy Mountain.

In the next year, in the town of Târgovişta
the people put Ceauşescu and Madame Elena
against a wall and pulled the triggers
for pretending they knew where Sugarcandy Mountain was.

Now Moses the Raven has come again,
this time he's wearing a stars-and-stripes waistcoat
telling the people he knows the way to Sugarcandy Mountain.

But what he doesn't say is that it's far above the clouds,
in the land of Nevermore.

Stormtroopers Repelled

I heard the rain as it jackbooted across my roof;
watched as the sky donned its uniform of iron-grey
and as the storm mapped out its dark conquests
over the pastels of my garden.

But, in time a lighter cloud lifted its white flag
in a quiet corner of the heavens.
A brave patch of blue marched forward
and, freed, claimed its golden medal from the afternoon.

Causeway of the Legion .

Hanging reality
on the nine-foot menhir of Maen Madog
(*Dervacius filius Iusti hic iacit*),
your twenty-first century footsteps
lead you back through time,
down the path of Sarn Helen,
Sarn-y-lleng, causeway of the legion.

Half-seen, half-imagined,
through the damp mists of November
shadows might be the cohorts of Rome,
weary and wet from their fording
of the headwaters of the Neath.

Do the lined faces of the Squaddies or GIs of their day
show hawkish contempt for their Imperial conquests?
Do they use the native girls roughly,
a light diversion for soldiers on the march?

Or does some rheum
in the corners of their eyes
speak of a search for the sunlit uplands
of their Sienna homes?
Does it tell that they know of their unwelcome,
these strangers in a strange land,
and that they are as anxious to escape from
their own troubled times
as I am from mine?

1952: The Year of Yellow Frankie

The canal flowed through my early life;
that dark forbidden place at the end of my street.
I wondered what my mother meant when she said:
'little Frankie was yellow when they pulled him out.'

Why did my friend share the hue of the dandelions
blowing fairy-seeds across the wasteland we called 'the dump',
a place almost as outlawed as the canal that ran through it;
a place where giants and gypsies spirited children away.

A few weeks after, escaping from the haven of my garden,
I clambered, circus-style, across the pipe that spanned the canal.
I was four then; it seems like a death-defying feat to me now.
You could say I was lucky
I didn't end up as yellow as little Frankie.

Later, in wiser years, I learned to angle for roach and perch.
I found that the canal was only six feet deep;
that there were no giants; gypsies were harmless travelling folk;
seeds of the yellow dandelion were not infant fairies.

But, sometimes, in the gathering murk,
I screwed my eyes at my yellow float,
a darkening tie between depthless water and firm land,
and remembered little Frankie.

Now, there are luxury homes on that giant's playground.
The canal is sleek and well-tended;
a place where people cruise their yellow pleasure boats;
no space for gypsies near this expensive land.

Still, I wonder if some small wraith of no colour now
drifts into those luxury homes
on nights of a yellow moon,
looking for the grandchildren that might have been.

Does this spirit look to give a warning
of that place of yellow death?
Or do the small ones hunch further over their video games?
And am I the only one who still remembers
my mother's words from nineteen fifty-two?

Prayer Requests at St Saviours

Dartmouth. Rain. Hiding in a church.
Scribbles on Post-it notes:

For my dear sister Myfanwy.
For Mum, that she may find her way out of confusion.
For Aunt Peggy's legs.

Where's the harm?

That Uncle John's pain may ease.
For Granny in her trials.

Then one note, all alone.

For all the people in this wonderful world of ours.

The Royal Pavilion, Brighton

These are the tatters of a once-glittering onion, built
by the gross son of a mad king.
The people pay their ten pounds to gawp at the opulence
or listen, hushed, to prayers to consumption
over headsets obtained at the door.

The banqueting room is the worst;
silver plates, cut glass and gold candlesticks
set amid Chinoiserie and Mughal fancies.
The kitchen gives some relief,
despite arrays of brass pans once wielded
by half-starved scullions.

Then, a menu from 1817:
fifty-six dripping courses of game and gout.
More than a family would see in a lifetime.

The music room brings peace at first.
Once there'd be Handel and Rossini.
Now all you hear is
whispered invitations to fall down and worship
echoing in twenty pairs of tourist ears.

What are they thinking,
those who come to pray at this shrine?
Are they grateful
they're not Georgian peasants?
Or do they wish their name was George?

It was too much for me;
what was I doing here?

Tom East

I backtracked, clickety-clacking
my suitcase behind me.
There was horror on the
faces of the circulating crowd
as I noisily defiled
their cathedral to wealth.

'Are we looking for the way out, Sir?'
asked a suit of shiny silver buttons.
            You bet I was.

The Secret Society

The deck of the *Amorique* near sunset,
mid-Channel, mid-October.
The Sun nudges behind a cloud.
Cool becomes colder as the wind rises.
It is then the secret society emerges:
a shivering woman in woebegone middle age,
long-legged in her leather-fringed skirt.
A boy with bulging eyes,
bonily half-filling his flimsy green tee shirt.
A man with a snivelling nose,
pretending he's out for a stroll.
Others drift less memorably around the deck.
Then, wind-wrinkled fingers delve for concealed treasures,
furtive glances are exchanged.
Deep sighs of satisfaction surface
as a dozen small glows dance success.
Isn't it good not to smoke these days?

Scenes from a Season of Madness

[I] Idyll above the Rhondda Fach, 1922

Bwgi wakes on the mountain side,
looks about for stone-throwing children,
and reaches for his stick.
Breathing his magic into it,
he makes music only he can hear:
A-Bobble A-Bobble A-Bobble;
Y Phobl Y Phobl Y Phobl.
Music that gives life a meaning
until the magic fades;
until the stick is stick once more;
until stone-throwing starts again
and Bwgi sleeps upon the mountain.

[II] Diagnosis: Cephalalgia

Yellow electric beams, sodium and steel,
needle-stitch a tapestry behind the eyes.
Four dimensons; not one of them your own.
Every step a step down the spiral stair.
White coats, white ceilings, white pills
shimmer through the closing shadows:
welcome to the front row of the Theatre of Psyche.

III. Old Bedlam

Passing by the Bedlam door
you'll see black dogs in the straw.
We do trepanning with lobotomy,
for those who don't like straight leucotomy.
Then these purgatives from purgatory
with decoctions of antimony
or cupped glasses and blood-letting
for those who persist in their bed-wetting.

Try a good old-fashioned caning,
even padlocks and a chaining,
or a harness and swing-chair,
iron collars and well-shaved hair.
So once inside, this door's for locking.
Electrodes make things really shocking

[IV] New Bedlam

I'll have some Thisozine and Thatozine
a sleepy-pill and wakey-pill.
Come on Doctor, don't be mean –
I tell you now I'm really ill.

One to help me through the night,
one to ease my mortal pain,
one to teach me wrong from right,
one to help me clear my brain.

I like their rattle in the dish,
their colours promise every wish.
There's magic there beyond description
so fill me out my new prescription.

[V] Tightrope

How to walk this jagged wire?
Strike out boldly in the darkness,
stroke the black dog,
tell him he's your friend?

Or shrivel in the corner,
turn on the blinding light,
keep all dogs on a lead,
sing a song of sixpence,
pray for a quiet end?

Michael Maine and the Demon of Youth

Michael Maine (that's not his real name)
was not the most popular boy in our class.
Nondescript. Retiring. A bit dim really.

Not like John Horton, Ben Maple or Chris Wolfe.
(They're not their real names).
They were destined for great things:
one's a financial whiz; one became a senior civil servant;
another is an architect. Don't know about the rest.
Especially Michael Maine (not his real name).

One day, after hours, these good boys leaped on him,
electric shock machine poised in readiness.
They wrestled him to the ground,
which wasn't so hard really:
not much of a fighter was Michael Maine (not his real name).

Like the others there, I added to the throng,
pressing forward to see what this youthful Diablo was planning
for Michael Maine (not his real name).

Or I might have been thinking of my head-case reputation;
or that it wouldn't protect me – I might have been next,
after Michael Maine (not his real name).

They removed his trousers and his pants – a curious yellow –
to show his tiny testicles, small and polished –
a quarter of the size they should have been.
Poor Michael Maine. That's not his real name.

It didn't seem right to me
but still I said nothing, did nothing,
even when they attached the electrodes to
the small member of Michael Maine – not his real name.

He twitched in the air when they switched it on,
and then lay for a while, hideously still,
as the demon left the room,
leaving boys to become boys again.
We went about our business, hushed.
No one said anything to Michael Maine – not his real name.

Michael Maine. That's not his real name.
But I know what his real name was.

Alchemy

The quest: to transform base metal into gold.
He closes his eyes to fire, earth and water:
snake's tongue and seed of nightshade concern him now.

Farewell blue canopy, hail black cellar.
Human bonds unloose in straining after mystery.

Shadows lengthen on the wall.
A life, once quick, becomes dust.

Alchimie

Căutara: să preschimbi metalul de rând în aur.
Inchide ochii la foc, pământ şi apă:
limba şarpelui şi sămânţa de zirnă îl obsedează acum.

Rămas bun, boltă albastră, salut, pivniţă întunecată.
Legăturile-omeneşti slăbesc în sforţarea de-a afla misterul.

Umbrele se lungesc pe ziduri.
O viaţă, cândva plină, se preface-n colb.

(traduceara din limba engleză de dr. Petru Iamandi)

Summer on the Planet Mars

Summer on the Planet Mars;
    no flowers bloom upon the heath –
the hand of time has left its scars.
Summer on the Planet Mars –
the hand of man his home besmears,
    brings Martian clime to Planet Earth.
Summer on the Planet Mars –

no flowers bloom upon the heath.

Nun on the National Health

At five o'clock she tells her beads.

They couldn't quite understand
why this nun of ninety years
must have her *Steradent* on the table
while she makes her devotions.

And surely it's not the normal thing
to say *Hail Marys* lying on one's back
on the floor of the public ward this way?
'No,' says Mother Superior,
'But we can't cope with her in the convent now'.

Seven o'clock, breakfast time.

She says 'Goodnight';
exchanges habit for ward dressing gown,
and soon the afterglow of the nut-brown smile
is framed by the gospel white of the hospital pillow.

Eight o'clock: may the Light of the World be with her.

Scenes from a Season of Foxhunting

[I] Freedom

Freedom is within you
someone said.
He was a foxy guy
in a coat of red.

[II]Fox Free

I am

        I am

I am

        I am

Fox Free

I am

You raised me
from a cub. So
why are you ripping
me apart, you bast --

[III] D'ye Ken?♪

To THAT tune, allegretto, alla marcia
D'ye ken this man in his coat so red?
He smells like the hounds that he's oft-times led.
He doesn't think like us so we'll pass a law instead
and stop his fun without war-ning.
So don't tell me that you'd rather stay in bed,
for the sound of *The Quorn* would awaken the dead
or even poor Tony Blair in the mor-ning.

[IV]Seeing off the Llangeinor Hunt

On any St. Stephen's Day
you will see the village of Blackmill
seeing off the Hunt.
See the village off I say!
Pass a law against them all!
See, it's easy.

[V] Blessed be the Lawmakers

Smoking in public parks?
Make them stub their devil-sticks out.
Skinned live frogs in buckets?
We won't go there again.
Fox-hunting?
Sharpen your pencils.
La Corrida in Spain?
Reach for the bombs.

[VI]Freedom Revisited

Freedom is within you
someone said.
He was very wise
or off his head.

Milwaukee Lady Makes Number Thirty-eight

All I wanted was to swim a length or two,
but she snared me with her monologue:
the folks back home; her seventy-five years;
this summer-long tour; the foibles of the others;
her life with Elmer – or was it Homer?
(Long departed, leaving his dollars here).
How proud she was of her catalogue of lands;
that's thirty-seven now, more next year.
She said she was to visit Wales: 'is that a country then?'
'Why,' she murmured, pulling off with elegant stroke,
'that's number thirty-eight'.

Meeting the East Hill Mob

One wet night I met the East Hill Mob,
or, should I say, they introduced themselves with a bottle,
shattering on the road six feet behind me.
Too proud or too stupid to run,
I watched the ring of faces.
Seemed they were at more of a loss than me,
till someone took it into his head to throw a punch.

Later, when I was down, being kicked on the floor,
it felt more like a ritual than a beating.
It didn't hurt much beyond my pride:
a graze on the cheek, a bootprint on a shirt.

The graze faded, the shirt was washed,
pride healed itself; it always does.
And yet the drunken whoop in the street;
the Saturday-night scream;
the chorus of cat-calls;
make a different music to me now.
And, on a bad day, in some dark corner of my mind,
still lurks the menace of the boot-boy.

Perhaps the shirt wasn't washed as clean as I thought.

The Bottle Factory

Looking back, I'll say I liked it,
that year I spent among the glass.
A model dark satanic mill as ever was.

The ragtime note of steel on glass;
the hot breath of the friendly furnace;
the march of bottles from the lehr –
all have, remembered, special charm.

Bottles green and brown and blue,
hot to touch and sometimes broken –
even now I bear the scar.

The men were men, the bosses bastards,
but bosses of your hands, not souls.
A simple deal, a neat equation:
pay for sweat, your mind your own.

I liked best to start the night shift
full of beer, a drunken star,
and after just an hour of working
I'd sweated sober, unconcerned.

Then at seven in the morning
the hooter sang out our release,
so off we marched to seek our freedom
and, as for me, I'm searching still.

Gawain the Goude

Even now, after many seasons passing,
as he passes through the seasons,
I am mazed by this gentlyest knyght.

I see him spurn the lady's cors,
forsake the lel layk of luf,
to cross the freezing fells,
for his lamb at Cristes Masse.

Yet I do forgive him that,
so clene in his courte.
But when he takes the green girdle,
the luf lace of the lady,
and casts it to the ground,
I know him to be mad.

The Fat Lady's Victory

She joined the train at Pontyclun,
huffing and puffing, clinically large.
Anxious pop-eyes looked around: no seat.
Never was one more needed.

Close by a cosy four-seater,
taken by just two – hikers, bikers, young and free,
their army-camp of bags, bottles and boots
strewn around their careless territory.

She cast a longing glance in their direction,
deep sighs came from her bulk
as she and the train lurched and staggered
through the steaming darkness of the night.

We looked on at this silent drama
being played before our eyes.
Some crisis; perhaps a medical collapse we thought,
but no-one spoke, no-one moved.

Face grew redder, breathing strained.
We feared that the large and trembling legs
could barely hold the larger frame
decked about with shopping-bags.

Then, when it seemed that she would burst,
with one last effort she shambled forward,
smiled the smile of the fair young girl that once she was,
and in that moment won her victory.

Boots and bottles made way for Tesco shopping-bags
as this Queen of the Hour enthroned herself
and all around we smiled, drew easy breath again,
untouched and safe in our own little islands.

Eleven-liner

Every line must rhyme, you tell me from your eminence.
        That's the way to be sublime;
if you want to strive for excellence,
        every line must rhyme.

        But I think that it's a crime
when a roundel cries for assonance
        to make a poem, not a chime.

So I hope you understand, when I ask you in my innocence
        why is it, each and every time,
when aim should be best cadence,
        every line must rhyme?

Let Them Eat Cake

Let them eat cake,
but only wholesome cake with crunchy organic bits.
Let them not eat chips
(*oh no, not the chips*),
greasy burgers, sticky buns
or anything of that kind.
Let them wet their lips
with nothing but the purest water.
No fizzy drinks, strong sweet tea
and definitely no lager in cans.
Pulses, nuts and fruit
should be subsidised.
The purest white robes
(with no hood)
should be the standard apparel
for the lower orders.
They should be made to carry a handbell
to ring loudly when they
really have to walk through our walled areas.
Let them… wait, don't we need to make economies?
They're all in this together:
let them die.

Charley Bates

Charley Bates? Who's he?
Ah, The Dodger's flag man.
A larrikin of Fagin the Kidsman,
like so many others.

He was a little snakesman down in The Smoke;
lifting swag and wipes from a gropus,
chancing being lagged and the drop,
like so many others.

He was a rookery rat,
a tugger, a fine wirer,
a hoister, a dipper, a gonoph for the gilt,
like so many others.

Today, we'd use other expressions:
damaged, maladjusted,
in need of care and attention,
like so many others.

At the end of the story,
he worked his way up to respectability.
But then, he breathed only in the pages of fiction,
like so many others.

Windowscape

Time and the early morning train had stopped.
The neon morning took on a softer glow
to enjoy this gifted freedom from the workaday world.
Even the buzzing voices of others in the carriage
dropped by a respectful octave: they sensed it, too.

Glass and steel sealed us within.
Outside was a watercolour December
under a cloud-and-ink sky.
Even the distant orange street lights
barely intruded on this quiet moment.

Car headlights were the eyes of faraway ghosts.
Some flying creature shadowed past the window,
its quest no business of ours.
Silhouettes of trees were the cardboard scenery
of the stage outside.

Then the signal changed;
over the speaker a hesitant apology,
and the train grumbled forward.
Talk was all of minutes lost from the business day,
but in the secret place lingered a passing regret
that the clocks were ticking again.

Scenes from a Season in Malaysia

[I] Fireflies, River Selangor

'Kami akan berada disini sampai pukul satu'
-       *'We could be out here until one o'clock'.*
That's what you said, in your giggling Malay
as you rowed the sampan up and down, from side to side.
It seemed we had plenty of time, too,
underneath the pin-pricking stars, thunder away in the distance.

Then we saw them, around the river's bend:
the host of Christmas tree lights,
each one a gleam of life,
flashing their mating hopes at each other.

The sampan still cruised up and down, side to side,
lazing its way across the still waters,
as you gave your biology lesson, lost on me.
It would have been in any language –
my senses open only to the night, the stars and the cool river.

Then you said that the builders would move in soon:
another shopping complex or condominium needed here.
Perhaps there is not as much time as we thought.
The thunder grumbled more closely now.

[II] Central Bus Station, Kuala Lumpur

So why should she look at me that way,
        when other bus-station beggars let me be?
They ask no more than a little pay:
        so why should she?

        She can't blame her twisted shape on me,
and though I see her with dismay,
        it's not my fault, her vagrancy.

The leprous Hindu, the old Malay,
    they're only after some buckshee,
don't seek to wrench my soul away:
    so why should she?

[III] Mudskippers

Mudskippers don't skip;
they slither wetly between mud-pools.
Or at least they do in Melaka harbour,
as they quarrel, dwarf dragons in their moist empires.

As you look down on these strange lizard-gobies
from the height of decaying wood piles
you wonder if these creatures have come to the end of the road
of their evolutionary dead end.

But if they could see us
through their goggle eyes,
what would they wonder about us?

Would they say we quarrel noisily above the wood-piles?
Have we reached our evolutionary dead end?

Twilight Owl

Your round eyes dazzled by our headlights,
we saw you there; a surprised sentinel on a gatepost.
Indignant, you fluffed up your feathers,
gave an angry shake of your form,
and then twisted your head,
closing our electric-gliding boat
from your sight and from your world.

It was only twin carelessnesses of time
that had brought our moments together.
The stars had yet to climb in the sky;
the sun had long since fallen to the west.

Soon, a bend in the canal
banished these intruders from the daytime realm.
You would soon spread strong wings,
bringing dark fear to the crawling creatures,
and we would moor, cursing in the gloom.

As we arced round the cut, I strained to hear your ghostly call.
None came: we had been dismissed from your hunter's mind.
But for a moment, I wondered about you.
Could it be that, somewhere off in the drear dark,
tearing shrews and water-voles for your brood,
or regally retching animal bones and fur,
you wondered about us, too?

♪ Blue Treen Blues ♪

I'm not the baddest Venusian you ever seen,
yeah, I'm really down an' I'll tell you why.
I'm lanky, I'm lipless, I'm sure as Mars lean,
But green? Why, I'm blue as that ole' Earth-sky.

Yeah, I'm so blue I'm not green:
got the Blue Treen Blues.

They say there's no palette bar in this place,
but I seen them signs on the doors:
'*No smilies. No lippies. If you're blue it's disgrace.*'
Aquas like me can go sleep on the floors.

Yeah, I'm so blue I'm not green:
got the Blue Treen Blues.

That Ole' Mekon, he jus' says to annoy,
from way up there on his flying dinner-plate:
'Why aintcha like your green brothers, boy?
You in some kinda azure state.'

Yeah, I'm so blue I'm not green:
got the Blue Treen Blues.

Dan Dare, that pilot, he got no future with me,
an' that Digby mus' be on some kinda trip.
Man, they sure funny and pink, Lordie be –
but *they* can go back on the next rushin' wind ship.

Yeah, I'm so blue I'm not green:
got the Blue Treen Blues.

NOTES

[1] The Venusian adversaries of Dan Dare, 'pilot of the future' in the *Eagle*
comic of the ninteen-fifties and sixties were 'the Treens'. They had green skin
and their leader was 'The Mekon'.
[2] The first important immigrant ship from the West Indies was *The Empire
Windrush*.

Farmer on a Scooter

[With Apologies to RS Thomas for taking liberties with **Cynddylan on a Tractor***]*

Ah, you should see this gentleman in the fields.
Gone the old ways that seated him on a tractor;
he's a new man now, part of the money-machine.
His nerves are metal as the farmhands toil.
They may curse but still must obey
his least bidding or, lo, they're away,
these scattered Czechs and Poles, with no pay,
out of the country, back to their Eastern friends.
He rides his scooter, as a farmer should;
no need now for him to break the fields.
Why labour on the soil, when others should?
Spreadsheets and grant forms fill his days;
he has a bank manager to please.
The sweated brow is not for him –
his business now runs on a different fuel;
these zero-hours contracts are a boon.
Once around the field then home to count his gain,
as he drives his scooter proudly up the lane.

Brynhyfryd

My pilgrimage to the Aman Valley,
was made with a camera,
as if the boyhood home
of this poet of Wales
was the Taj Mahal or the Pyramids.

I stood before blackened walls
as if revering a shrine,
not a mean terraced house like the others.
I hesitated to click the shutter;
a woman stepped out.

In a Polish accent, she questioned:
had her landlord had sent me?
Was I on a mission to cast her in the gutter?

Is this what we've come to?
Do I look like a bailiff?
Has the high quarried ledge
become an escape for economic migrants?

But pause: Grandsire Job Lewis was just that.
He sought light under the mountain over Aberdare
away from the quarry-masters of Llywn'rebol,
the gracious Masters of Efail Wen who wouldn't pay
their men for six weeks of toil.

Perhaps the jaded dust of this house
is a shrine, and the chippings of stones in Egypt or India
are shrines to the lives of the anonymous men who died
erecting monuments to their masters.

Crow

Out of an October sky he came,
a black-skirted dancer, far from his home.
 Between hard-stepping, impatient feet
 he weaved his quest for a feast;
scraps left by human whim.

He found it: a bag of half-eaten treasure
and, spreading fine feathers,
 took to the air, his prize clamped in a dark beak
 leaving those feet to their strange trudge.
His were different pleasures:

   To thrill his crow-home.
   To fill his crow-women.
   To shrill his crow-laugh.

I smiled at this winged spread of oil;
this crow-ward flight of cholesterol.
 although I could tell from the glint in his bright eye
 that I was seeing the highlight of his day.
This was a crow-festival.

Lunch in Bosnia

The Meal

They called it a local dish:
Dolmo is Greek Dolmades by another name;
a slice of kebab adds some flesh;
stuffed peppers taste the same, Adriatic or Mediterranean;
anywhere in Eastern Europe serves corn mash;
rice could as well go with roast lamb.
Baklava and Turkish tea make a finish.

The Town

In Mostar, once capital of Hercegovina
tourists cross the symbolically rebuilt East-West bridge.
The blood has been washed from this arena
but bullet holes in buildings are worn like a badge,
a reminder of nearby Saravejo, where the Archduke died
while The Black Hand smiled.

The People

Serbian Orthodox,
Croatian Catholic,
Bosnian Muslim,
Greek, Jew, Albanian, Turk and more.
Stir and shake as you like
but not too hard.
It's been done before.

The War

'The Homeland War': a friendly sound.
Serbia pushed into Croatia,
Croatia held its ground
and Bosnia was a handy location
for some ethnic cleansing
that will take some mending.

The peace

    Bosnia is slower to recover
    than neighbours to south and north.
    But on a sunlit day in early May,
    smiles told of coming rebirth.
    The firm, egalitarian handshake of a waiter
    might have said it was time for brother to embrace brother.

Conger

Like all good intentions,
a conger eel starts life as a leptocephalus.
> A thread of quicksilver,
> fragile and innocent in the sea.

The eel drifts in the ocean
> metamorphosing, taking solid form,
> growing dark in body,
> growing sharp in tooth.

Sometimes the conger finds a mark,
some kind of jetsam or wreck,
and grows rich on the fat of the seas.

Its meals brought to its mouth by the flow,
the creature grows ever larger,
until it grows so large
that it gets trapped
in the feeding-lair that grew it.

♪ Special Relationship Blues ♪

With apologies to Spencer Williams for taking liberties with *Basin Street Blues*

Won't you come along with me
Down that old Euphratee-ee
We'll take our tanks to the land of dreams:
Come along with me; you know what it means.

I'm tellin' ya, we got a special relationship,   [CHORUS]
Just watch me shoot, straight from the hip,
In Old Baghdad, the land of dreams -
You'll never know how much it means
That we gotta special relationship.

We'll be shootin' and a-killin'
Shame them Frenchie boys just ain't willin'
An' all them guns ... Lordie, if you just listen
You know what it means ... yeah Special Relationship Blues.
[CHORUS]

[INSTRUMENTAL BREAK]

Now you'll be glad you went with me
Down that wandrin' Euphratee.
We'll take our tanks to the land of dreams:
It's *essential* ... yeah, we got a special relationship.

Recent Fiction by Tom East:

The Eve of St Eligius

The Greenland Party

Tommy's War: July, 1914

Coming Soon:

The Gospel According to St Judas

Printed in Great Britain
by Amazon

17785047R00051